The Llangollen Round

An exhilarating high-level walk
encircling the picturesque
Vale of Llangollen

Published by The Llangollen Round Association
ISBN 978-0-9568184-0-9

Text and map : Judy Smith
Photos : Judy Smith and Trevor Jefferies
Photos of raptors on pages 6 & 7 by kind permission of Linda Wright
Profiles : Bill Saunders
Typesetting & layout : Red Dog Books (www.reddogbooks.com)

Printed by imprint*digital*.net

If you need any advice regarding this route, do not hesitate
to contact us at
The Llangollen Round Association
Ty'n Llechwedd, Dinbren, Llangollen LL20 8EB
Tel 01978 869364
e-mail : thellangollenround@gmail.com
Website www.thellangollenround.info

Llangollen Committee of Cancer Research UK are indebted to Judy Smith, whose inspiration and hard work led to the creation of the Llangollen Round and the production of this booklet. They are also very grateful to Harold Mewes of Red Dog Books for all his time and expertise so generously given. More thanks are due to Trevor, Angela, Bill and Eric for their much-valued contributions to this project

CONTENTS

Planning your walk

This description divides the Llangollen Round into 6 sections determined by the places at which it is most accessible (see p.12 & 13). It can be started at any of those places and theoretically, it can even be done in reverse. Not everyone can or would want to complete the whole 33 miles in a day. Suggestions for taking it at a more leisurely pace are:-

2 days: Day 1, sections A, B, C, and D (16 miles). Day 2, sections E and F (17 miles). **Or** (access by public transport) : Day 1, sections B, C, D, and E (18.4 miles). Day 2, sections F and A (14.6 miles)

3 days: Day 1, sections A, B and C (11.8 miles). Day 2, sections D and E (11.2 miles). Day 3, section F (10.0 miles)

4 days: Day 1, sections A and B (6.8 miles). Day 2, sections C and D (9.2 miles). Day 3, section E (7.0 miles). Day 4, section F (10.0 miles).

Route directions (below, and p.9 onwards) contain abbreviations:

CA = continue ahead   *L* = left   *R* = right   *SP* = signpost

N.B. 'left' and 'right' are abbreviated only when that direction is to be followed. All distances given are approximate.

Getting to and from the Round

The route forms a complete circle around Llangollen (see p.12 &13). From the town it can be accessed by bus at points 4 and 16 , by train at point 16, and by taxi at several points. On foot, points 1 and 6 are the most easily reached, both just under 2 miles from the town centre.

To access point 1 on foot: walk up Castle Street to the traffic lights and cross the A5 diagonally **L**. Continue up Hill Street (**SP** Plas Newydd), keep **L** at the top, then **L** again beside the entrance to Plas Newydd. The road dips to cross a stream then rises with the housing estate of Pengwern on the left. Shortly afterwards, past the de-restriction signs, take the 1st turn **R** (SP Glynceiriog) and climb steeply to the road junction at the top of the hill, which is point 1.

To access point 6 on foot: at the railway end of Llangollen Bridge, turn **R**, then immediately go **L** up Wharf Hill. After crossing the canal turn **R** and continue on this road for 1½ miles to the foot of the Eglwyseg rocks behind Castell Dinas Brân. Turn **R** here and at the fork shortly afterwards, keep **L**. In 1/3 mile the road bends **L** to the sharp corner at point 6.

Bus timetables can be obtained from www.wrexham.gov.uk/bus or by phoning 01978 266166. Buses pass point 4 approximately every 15 minutes and point 16 approximately every 2 hours.

Train timetables can be obtained from www.llangollen-railway.co.uk or by phoning 01978 860979. At weekends and holiday times there may be up to 6 trains a day between Llangollen and Carrog (point 16).

Telephone numbers of taxi firms can be obtained from **Llangollen Tourist Information**, who will also be happy to advise on all transport and accommodation options. Tel 01978 860828.

Before setting off, a few points to bear in mind –

The sketch map in this booklet should be sufficient to get you round, but you might also like to see the route on the appropriate Ordnance Survey maps – Explorers 255 and 256.

Walking in the mountains. This is a route rising above 600m and passing through areas that are quite remote. Remember it will probably be colder and windier on the heights. Also the weather can change quickly, so always carry an extra layer of clothing and waterproofs. Make sure you have enough food and water for the day and some emergency rations as well. Let someone know where you are going, or at least leave a note in your room.

Do not rely on your mobile phone because reception in these mountains can be patchy. It would be sensible to carry a whistle – the emergency signal is 6 loud blasts repeated at one minute intervals.

If in doubt about the weather you can get the most up to date Met Office information by calling Weathercall on 09068 500 415, and when prompted, entering the area code 1506. (The cost is 60p/minute but it may be money well spent.)

Restrictions on Open Access Land. Some parts of this walk cross Open Access Land, which landowners can close at any time for land management purposes. In practice, this very rarely happens, and where it does, there will always be diversion signs. Any advance notice of closure will be posted on the Llangollen Round website, www.thellangollenround.info.

On Open Access Land, dogs are required to be on a lead between 1st March and 31st July, to protect ground-nesting birds.

THE NATURAL ENVIRONMENT

UNDER YOUR FEET. A large part of this walk is on heather moorland. The thin peaty soil supports three types of heather – *ling, bell heather* and *cross-leaved heath*. The latter two are reasonably similar, with bell-like purple flowers on spikes, but the woody, springy, lighter-coloured ling is by far the most common. All the heathers flower in late summer and if you visit at this time you will be treated to a dazzling carpet of purple.

Gorse and bilberry thrive alongside the heather, while silver birch and rowan sparsely dot the open landscape. Bracken is a somewhat unwelcome invader of the scene.

Heather moorland needs to be 'managed' – it needs to be burned or cut every few years to encourage regeneration, and you will see obvious patches in the landscape where this has been done.

Wildlife on the moors includes mice and voles, the natural prey of raptors. Red grouse are also present, and will catapult into the air with a whirring sound when disturbed. In recent years the rarer Black Grouse has returned to these uplands.

OVER YOUR HEAD. The high moorland is home to a variety of raptors. Buzzards are common, soaring high on rounded 'fingered' wings. The smaller Hen Harriers fly low on wings held in a 'V', while the forked tail of the rare Red Kite makes it easily distinguishable. Of the smaller falcons, the hovering kestrel is easy to spot, while the Peregrine and the Merlin are rarer, and are both protected species. The Peregrine is a great 'diver', dropping from the sky upon its prey, while the Merlin flies low and arrow-like across the moorland.

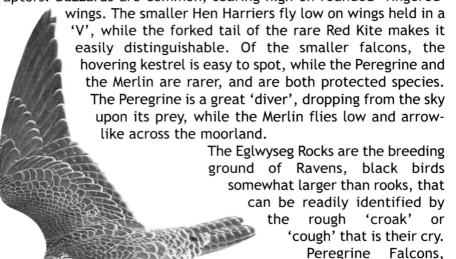

The Eglwyseg Rocks are the breeding ground of Ravens, black birds somewhat larger than rooks, that can be readily identified by the rough 'croak' or 'cough' that is their cry. Peregrine Falcons, too, are frequently seen in this area.

above: red kite
below left: kestrel
below right
(and opposite page):
peregrine falcon

THE LANDSCAPE

The River Dee flows east from Bala Lake to the sea beyond Chester and on its way passes through the Vale of Llangollen. On the south side of the Vale the mountains are the Berwyns, formed from sedimentary rock some 450 million years old. In places this ancient mudstone and siltstone has been compressed to give the local blue-grey slate, once so popular for roofing. The quarry you will pass on Moel-y-Faen is now closed, as is the one on Moel Fferna, but the nearby Berwyn Slate Quarry, on the lower flanks of Moel-y-Gamelin, is still operational.

North of the Dee, the Eglwyseg River divides Llantysilio Mountain and Cyrn-y-Brain from Ruabon Mountain. While the first two have similar origins to the Berwyns, Ruabon Mountain is geologically speaking much younger. A huge tilted block of carboniferous limestone (a mere 330 million years in age), it is overlaid by millstone grit, leaving the limestone strata only exposed along the edge of the escarpment as the 'Eglwyseg Rocks'. Since these rocks were once a reef in a tropical sea, they are teeming with the fossils of tiny marine creatures.

Above the rock strata, on the summit plateau of the Mountain, the scars of 18th and 19th century lead and zinc mining are visible, as are the grassed-over craters where bombs fell in the last World War. The

mountain was lit with flares at night as a decoy for enemy aircraft heading for Liverpool. And going way farther back in time, Ruabon Mountain also bears witness to prehistoric occupation, with a scattering of cairns, standing stones, and tumuli.

Trevor Rocks

Section A
Top of the Gwernant to Wrexham Road
4.6 miles

Point ① to point ④
Grid Ref SJ 225398 to Grid Ref SJ 264423

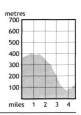

This is the most complicated section to navigate, but the going is largely very easy, and there are some outstanding views. After descending through woods to the village of Froncysyllte you cross Telford's famous aqueduct, 126 feet above the River Dee – and there is an alternative for those who would rather not.

This route description begins where the Gwernant, a narrow road ascending steeply from Llangollen, joins the minor road from Glynceiriog to Froncysyllte ①. Head east from here (L if you have come up the Gwernant, straight on if you have come from point ⑳), passing two radio masts on the left, and soon afterwards, a field that is used by a hang-gliding and para-gliding club. After almost 2 miles on this road a fork is reached ②.

Near the masts there are views south-east across Shropshire to the isolated mound of the Wrekin. When the view opens out on the opposite side, the tiered Trevor Rocks, southern outpost of the Eglwysegs, dominate the scene. Ahead below you is Froncysyllte with its aqueduct, while to the right lies the Cheshire Plain, broken by the Peckforton Hills. Far back left are the lofty summits of Llantysilio Mountain. Half the Llangollen Round is under your gaze.

At the fork ② take a track on the L, then in 50m cross a stile on the R. Cross the field, looking for a metal gate in the lower fence. Beyond the gate a path descends steeply through bracken and gorse to a stile leading to a narrow road. Bear L on this and continue downhill for 400m before taking a footpath signed behind a house on the R. This strong path continues along the edge of a wood, skirts the rim of a quarry, then descends to a narrow metalled road beside houses. Cross the road to the track opposite and in 20m, go over a stile on the R (in front of a radio aerial). The path now drops steeply through woodland to reach a residential road in Froncysyllte. Turn L and then bear R to descend Methodist Hill to the A5 ③.

Cross to Gate Road opposite, and immediately take the road on the R to drop to the Llangollen Canal. Cross the lift bridge (or the footbridge), turn L on the towpath to join the Offa's Dyke Path National Trail, and cross the aqueduct. At the end of the aqueduct, turn R to take a path passing underneath it.

(For more information about the aqueduct, call in at the Information Centre about 50m from its end, on the R, just beyond where the path turns to go underneath.)

(To avoid this high crossing altogether, CA on Gate Road at point ③, then bear R after the river bridge to rejoin the route.)

(Refreshments are available at the Anglo-Welsh boat hire base and at the Telford Inn, both near the end of the aqueduct.)

Coming out at the road bear R, cross the canal, and then turn L on a path above it. Cross the iron canal bridge, continue along the towpath, and cross back at the next bridge. Cross the field and pass under the old railway line. Turn R on a track that leads to the A539 Wrexham Road ④.

(A bus stop is 50m to your right here. There is a bus service to Llangollen every 15 minutes until about 6.30pm, with buses hourly thereafter until 9pm approx.)

View across the
Cheshire Plain

Pontcysyllte Aqueduct,
completed in 1805,
now has World
Heritage status.
Telford designed a
1000 ft long cast-iron
trough supported by
19 hollow pillars to
span the Dee Valley at
a height of 126 feet.
The plates of the
trough were packed
together with Welsh
flannel boiled in sugar,
and the stones of the
pillars were cemented
with bull's blood and
lime.

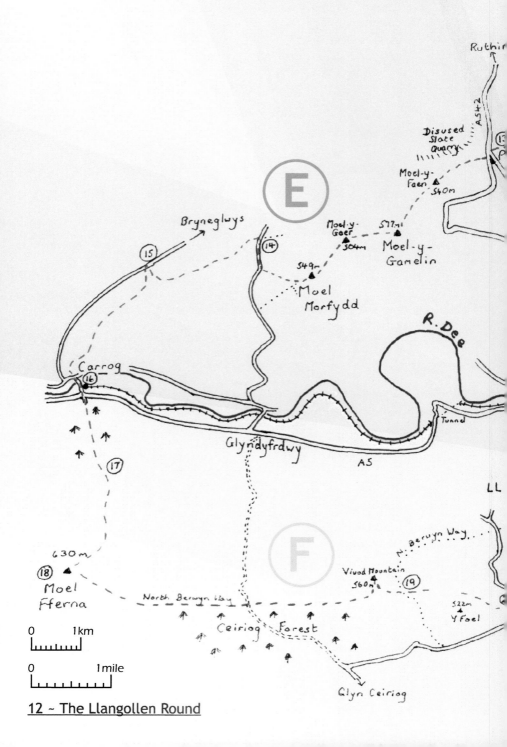

Ruthir

A5+2

Disused
Slate
Quarry

13
P

Moel-y-
Faen ▲
540m

E

Bryneglwys

Moel-y-
Goer ▲
504m

577m ▲

Moel-y-
Gamelin

15

14

549m ▲

Moel
Morfydd

R.Dee

Carrog

16

Tunnel

Glyndyfrdwy

A5

LL

17

F

N.Berwyn Way

630m

Vivod Mountain
560m ▲

19

18 ▲

Moel
Fferna

North Berwyn Way

Ceiriog Forest

522m
Y Foel

Glyn Ceiriog

0   1km
|‚‚‚‚‚‚‚|

0   1mile
|‚‚‚‚‚‚‚‚‚‚|

12 ~ The Llangollen Round

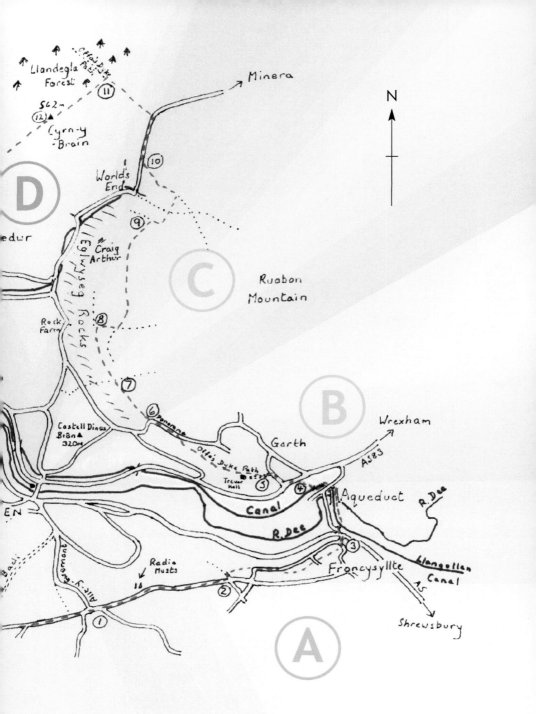

N

Llandegla Forest

Minera

562m
Cyrn-y-Brain

World's End

Craig Arthur

Eglwyseg Rocks

Rock Farm

Ruabon Mountain

edur

D

C

B

Wrexham

A483

Castell Dinas Brân 320m

Panorama

Offa's Dyke Path

Garth

Trevor Hall

Canal

Aqueduct

R.Dee

R. Dee

R. Dee

EN

Radio Masts

Froncysyllte

Llangollen Canal

A5

Shrewsbury

A

above: Castell Dinas Bran from the Panorama.

right: gate into Trevor Woods.

below: track onto the mountain from the Panorama.

Section B
Wrexham Road to Panorama junction
2.2 miles

Point ④ to point ⑥
Grid Ref SJ 264423 to Grid Ref SJ 235432

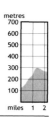

This short section, entirely on the Offa's Dyke Path, takes you uphill through Trevor Woods to a little road, known locally as the 'Panorama', running beneath the Eglwyseg Rocks. The road lives up to its name, with splendid prospects of precariously-sited Castell Dinas Brân, and Llangollen nestling in the valley below.

Turn L up the Wrexham Road. At the very top of the hill, take a road on the R (SP Offa's Dyke Path). In 400m, at a right-hand bend, CA on the track to Trevor Hall⑤. Go through the gate and in 30m take the signed path into woods on the R.

This path climbs steeply, passing a field on the right before plunging into coniferous woodland. CA, following Offa's Dyke signs, for just over a mile. The path then emerges from the trees and bends up alongside a house to reach the 'Panorama'. Turn L and enjoy the view.

Castell Dinas Brân was built on this curious hilltop around 1260. An Iron Age hillfort and a wooden fortress had previously occupied the site. The castle's builder was probably one Gruffydd II ap Madog, a marcher lord who held the wealthy territory of Powys Fadog between England and Wales. During Edward I's campaigns on the Welsh borders this stronghold soon came under threat, and while two of Gruffydd's sons sued for peace, others chose to burn down their castle rather than have it taken by the English. The splendid edifice had not lasted 20 years.

In 600m, leave the Panorama road at a sharp left-hand bend⑥ where a fingerpost points out a grassy track climbing ahead.

(Leave the Round at this point if you want to access Llangollen (1.8 miles) either by foot or by taxi. See Page 4 for details.)

Section C
Panorama junction to World's End
5.0 miles

Point ⑥ to point ⑩
Grid Ref SJ 235432 to Grid Ref SJ 232485

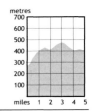

The path climbs steadily and very soon you are looking down on the ruins of Castell Dinas Brân, whose perch seemed so lofty from Llangollen town. Skirting the escarpment edge all the way, open heather moorland is reached, and there are magnificent views of the Clwydian Range stretching ahead. Look out for the curious mounds that are Bronze Age burial tumuli – and listen for the croak of ravens, and the high trills of hovering skylarks.

At the sharp bend, leave the Panorama and Offa's Dyke Path and CA up the broad grassy track, with a valley on your right. Soon pass left of a gate and CA outside the fence, with the edge of the escarpment away on the left. The path at length runs below the scattered trees of an old conifer plantation on the right to reach a path junction with a signpost ⑦.

CA here on the permissive path (left descends very steeply towards Llangollen, right goes across Ruabon Mountain). CA along the edge of the escarpment, passing through a gate beside a tumulus. After about a mile, at another marked path junction ⑧, turn R. Climb up the valley for about 200m to where a track crosses from the right behind. Follow it L, climbing the stony bank and maintaining the same direction across the uneven ground at the top, from where a clear grassy track opens out before you.

CA on this track heading north, and after a mile or so you will see Craig Arthur (Arthur's Rock), a low outcrop of limestone on the edge of the escarpment far away to the left.

Llangollen joins with much of the Celtic world in claiming connections with the King Arthur saga. These rocks were Arthur's seat, Castell Dinas

Brân briefly sheltered the Holy Grail, and the 9th century Eliseg's Pillar (in the valley below you) carried details of the chieftain Vortigern, whose advisor was the magician Merlin.

Eventually the path bends R descending to meet a much stronger path skirting the deep valley of World's End ⑨.

The rockface across the valley here is known as Craig-y-Forwyn (Maiden's Rock). The story goes that once upon a time a young girl rejected in love flung herself over the edge.

Turn R and follow the path around the rim of the valley. After it bends L a path crosses, and 300m later another signed path junction is reached. Turn L here, then at the fork take either path (they meet later) and CA down to the road above World's End ⑩.

(A small car park in the woodland 100m to your left makes a good pick up point for car or taxi. Llangollen 5 miles.)

on the moors above
World's End

Llantysilio Mountain from above World's End

Section D
World's End to Ponderosa
4.2 miles

Point ⑩ to point ⑬
Grid Ref SJ 232485 to Grid Ref SJ 192482

metres

Rejoining the Offa's Dyke Path, you follow it across moorland to the edge of Llandegla Forest. A short gentle climb leads to the radio masts on Cyrn-y-Brain (565m), and one of the most magnificent panoramas on the Round.

gate into Llandegla Forest

above: looking across the moor to Llandegla Forest
below: descending Cyrn-y-Brain to the Ponderosa

An easy track then descends to the Horseshoe Pass road (A542) where the Ponderosa Café awaits.

Turn R uphill on the road above World's End. In ½ mile, a roadside granite slab points L across the boggy moorland, where in places boardwalks have been laid.

Arriving at the forest edge ⑪, go through the double gate and immediately L on the stony track. Keep the fence on your left as far as the boundary of the forest, where a stile leads back on to the open moor. CA for 15 m (passing a faint path), then turn R up a track cleared through the heather and CA to the radio masts.

After you leave the forest, a stile in the fence gives access to a low mound of stones, all that remains of Sir Watkin's Tower. In the 18th century, wealthy local squire Sir Watkin Williams Wynn owned land in seven counties. He had the tower built at this spot, where all his domain was in view.

Pass the first radio mast, CA to the second and the nearby cairn. Pause to take in that fantastic view ⑫.

Start at nearby Llantysilio Mountain, directly ahead. Far back on its left are the sharp-edged Berwyns, Moel Sych, Cadair Berwyn and Cadair Bronwen. To the right of Llantysilio Mountain, the irregular shapes are the Arenigs, with conical Foel Goch nearer and between them. Moving clockwise you have distant Snowdonia, the closer Clwydians, and then the estuaries of the Dee and the Mersey (better seen from Sir Watkin's Tower). In the distance, the Peak District next lifts the horizon, followed by the Cheshire plain, broken by the line of Peckforton Hills. The circle completes with the humpbacked Wrekin, and finally the rounded silhouettes of the Shropshire Hills.

CA downhill on the concrete track to the road junction beside the Ponderosa ⑬.

(the Ponderosa does full meals and light snacks, open until approx 4pm in winter, later in summer.)

Section E
Ponderosa to Carrog Station
7.0 miles

Point ⑬. to point ⑯.
Grid Ref SJ 192482 to Grid Ref SJ 118435

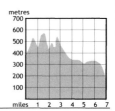

This is perhaps the most demanding section, taking in all the peaks that comprise Llantysilio Mountain. Moel-y-Faen (548m), Moel-y-

Gamelin (577m), Moel-y-Gaer (504m) and Moel Morfydd (549m) are crossed in quick succession, with wide-ranging views to reward your effort. From Morfydd the route descends steadily for 4 miles to reach the River Dee at Carrog.

top: Moel-y-Gamelin in late summer
centre left: ruins of Nant-y-Madwen
centre right: old greenroad beyond Nant-y-Madwen
bottom left: path along the moorland edge
bottom right: Carrog bridge

Walk up the road to the Ponderosa, then cross over to the rough parking area opposite. Take a clear grassy track that rises slightly to the left of you, and passes well left of the quarry edge. Climbing steadily, the track dips a little and becomes stony before it reaches the summit of Moel-y-Faen. CA over the summits of Moel-y-Gamelin, Moel-y-Gaer, and Moel Morfydd.

From a distance, Morfydd is easily identifiable by its 'notched' summit. Here at the top the two peaks are clear, one with a Trig. Pillar. There are impressive views all along the ridge, and for much of the way you can see directly down into the Vale of Llangollen.

Descending from Morfydd, take a path branching off to the R about 400m from the summit, just as the gradient becomes less severe (a post at the track entrance forbids motor cycles on the mountain). This twin-rutted track through the heather drops first gently, then more steeply, to a minor road. Turn R on the road and walk downhill as far as the cattle grid⑭.

Turn L in front of the cattle grid and follow the bridleway alongside the hedge. (You are now following the route of the Clwydian Way down to Carrog.)

Over the first stream bear L, and CA along the edge of the moorland with a fence on your right. Follow the path ahead, through a couple of gates, until after about a mile there is a gate into a field directly ahead. Go through, bearing R to find a grassy track going downhill between wall and fence to a narrow road⑮.

Turn L on the road, and in 30m, L again. Bear R up the field to a gate tucked behind a hedge corner. Through the gate you are on an ancient trackway that soon passes the ruins of Nant-y-Madwen farm, and then becomes more overgrown as it continues via gates and stiles along the hillside. In about a mile, where a track descends on the right, go over the stile into the field ahead and bear L beside the slate wall. Cross the next stile and descend directly, with the Dee valley now spread below you. After another stile you come to a fence beneath a fine chestnut tree. Turn R and drop steeply through woods to reach the Grouse Inn at Carrog. Walk down the road and over the river to the station ⑯.

(Carrog is 7½ miles from Llangollen. As an alternative to a taxi for your return, steam and/or diesel trains run regularly most days, with more frequent service at weekends and holidays. The last train is usually about 5.30pm. Carrog also has a 2-hourly bus service to Llangollen. The stop is 100m to the left on the A5.)

above: looking down on Carrog
left: Carrog station
below: stile at summit of Vivod Mountain

Section F
Carrog Station to Top of the Gwernant
10.0 miles

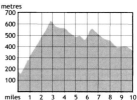

Point ⑯ to point ①
Grid Ref SJ 118435to Grid Ref SJ 225398

This section begins with a climb through the woods followed by a more gradual ascent of Moel Fferna, an outpost of the Berwyns. At 630m, this is the highest point of the Round, and the view is all you might expect. From Fferna the path crosses high moorland to the summit of Vivod Mountain, before descending to the top of the Gwernant, where this description of the Round began.

Walk up to the A5, cross it, and carry on up the road opposite, soon becoming a Forestry Commission track heading into Carrog Plantation. Where the track bears right, follow the yellow arrow (marked 'North Berwyn Way' - you are now on its 'Quarry Circuit') up the rough path L. At the next forest road, turn R then immediately L to a second forest road. Go R and L again and keep climbing on this broad track to reach a gravelled road. Once more, arrows take you climbing diagonally across it. Your track soon reaches the forest edge, then a gate on to the mountain ⑰. The summit of Fferna lies ahead and a little to the right.

Take the right-hand grassy track, marked by yellow arrows, up the side of a shallow valley. About ¾ mile from the gate, ignore a yellow arrow pointing ahead but turn off R on a wide, rutted, sometimes rather overgrown track leading to the summit ⑱.

The most striking feature of this stunning view is the nearby mass of the Berwyns (straight ahead), their highest point a mighty 200m above Fferna. With your back to the Berwyns the land dips away into the Dee valley – your eye can follow eastwards, but Llangollen is just out of sight. Beyond the Dee Valley are Morfydd, Gamelin, and Cyrn-y-Brain. Farther away still the Clwydians stand in line - even the highest of these (Moel Famau) is more than 75m below you. Turning in an anti-clockwise direction, the distant summits of Snowdonia come next, and on a clear day you can pick out Snowdon itself (at approx. 290°, if you have a compass). Anticlockwise again, the much nearer sharp-edged hump is that of Arenig. Finally, to the left of the Berwyns, just peeping behind the edge of a much nearer mountain, is the classically steep profile of the Breidden Hills near Welshpool.

At Fferna, you have joined the main route of the North Berwyn Way. Behind the cairn, cross to the fence and follow it L (do not cross the stile), continuing with the fence on your right. Descend for 1½ miles to the edge of the Ceiriog Forest. CA parallel to the fence, passing the gate, and soon cross the narrow road coming up from Glyndyfrdwy. Farther on the forest is left behind and the path climbs then bears L to reach the flat summit of Vivod Mountain (560m, 360° view). Cross the stile and turn R alongside the fence, descending with the 'Biddulph Tower' at the summit of Y Foel directly ahead.

At a marker post in a spinney of conifers ⑲, leave the North Berwyn Way and bear R, through a gate in the fence. Ignore the track ahead, but immediately turn L to continue with the fence on your left. CA for just over a mile along the flanks of Y Foel and finally, over a stile in a corner of fences, CA downhill through fields, keeping beside the fence, to meet a minor road near a junction ⑳.

Turn R, then L at the T-junction (the road from Glynceiriog to Froncysyllte). CA at each junction for 1½ miles to the top of the Gwernant ①.